DOG

YORKSHIRE TERRIERS

by Mary Ellen Klukow

AMICUS | AMICUS INK

Amicus High Interest and Amicus Ink are published by Amicus
P.O. Box 1329, Mankato, MN 56002
www.amicuspublishing.us

Library of Congress Cataloging-in-Publication Data
Names: Klukow, Mary Ellen, author.
Title: Yorkshire terriers / by Mary Ellen Klukow.
Description: Mankato, Minnesota : Amicus/Amicus Ink, [2020] | Series:
  Favorite dog breeds | Audience: K to Grade 3. | Includes index.
Identifiers: LCCN 2018030067 (print) | LCCN 2018032372 (ebook) | ISBN
  9781681517438 (pdf) | ISBN 9781681516615 (library binding) | ISBN
  9781681524474 (paperback)
Subjects: LCSH: Yorkshire terrier--Juvenile literature.
Classification: LCC SF429.Y6 (ebook) | LCC SF429.Y6 K58 2020 (print) |
  DDC 636.76--dc23
LC record available at https://lccn.loc.gov/2018030067

Photo Credits: iStock/zothen cover; iStock/tombaky 2; Shutterstock/
Susan Schmitz 5; iStock/Zocha_K 6–7; Alamy/yulia Petrova 8–9;
WikiCommons/Etching by J. Scott after A. Cooper. 10–11; Getty/Hill
Street Studios 12–13; iStock/gsagi 14; Getty/Khrystynabohush 16–17;
iStock/Laures 18–19; Shutterstock/tsik 21; iStock/GlobalP 22

Editor: Alissa Thielges
Designer: Ciara Beitlich
Photo Researcher: Holly Young

Printed in the United States of America

HC 10 9 8 7 6 5 4 3 2 1
PB 10 9 8 7 6 5 4 3 2 1

TABLE OF CONTENTS

PURSE DOGS

A tiny dog pokes its head out from a purse. It's a Yorkshire **terrier**! Yorkies love to go places with their owners. They are affectionate and happy.

YORKIE FUR

Yorkies have long tan and gray fur. It can be cut short. Yorkies are **hypoallergenic**. Their fur is like human hair. Most humans aren't allergic to Yorkies.

Furry Fact
The gray fur on Yorkies is called blue.

FEISTY AND STUBBORN

Yorkies are known for being **feisty**. They are sometimes hard to train. They are stubborn. They don't always listen. But they always love their owners.

THE RAT TRAP.

PEST CONTROL

Yorkies were bred by mixing other terrier breeds. They come from England. They were bred to be **pest controls**. They hunted rats.

Furry Fact
Yorkies are named after the county in England where they were bred, Yorkshire.

LAP DOGS

Yorkies became very popular in the late 1800s. They stopped hunting rats. They became **companion dogs**. They sat on people's laps all day.

Furry Fact
Owning a Yorkie in the 1800s was a sign of being rich.

BARKING

Yorkies bark a lot. They bark to ask for attention. They bark when a stranger knocks on the door. Some Yorkies are even used as **guard dogs**.

IN THE CITY

Yorkies are great city dogs. They can live in apartments. They like being around lots of people. Yorkies are the most popular breed in cities.

PUPPIES

Yorkies can have lots of puppies. Mother Yorkies can have ten puppies at once! Yorkie puppies are tiny. They weigh less than 1 pound (0.5 kg).

POPULAR PETS

Yorkies are great pets. Their endless energy makes them very playful. They are always up for a new adventure. No wonder they are so popular!

Furry Fact
Yorkies have been in the top 10 favorite dog breeds in America for the last five years.

HOW DO YOU KNOW IT'S A YORKSHIRE TERRIER?

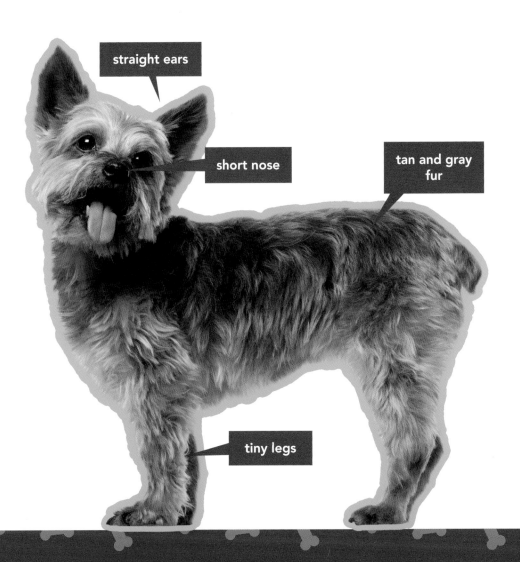

straight ears

short nose

tan and gray fur

tiny legs

WORDS TO KNOW

companion dog – a dog whose job is to love its owner

feisty – lively and sometimes aggressive

guard dog – a dog whose job is to protect its owner or home, sometimes just by barking

hypoallergenic – unlikely to cause an allergic reaction

pest control – something that kills pest animals like rats

terrier – a kind of dog bred to hunt down small, burrowing animals

LEARN MORE

Books

Frank, Sarah. *Yorkshire Terriers*. Minneapolis: Lerner Publications, 2019.

Gagne, Tammy. *The Dog Encyclopedia for Kids*. North Mankato, Minn.: Capstone Young Readers, 2017.

Pearson, Marie. *Yorkshire Terriers*. Lake Elmo, Minn.: Focus Readers, 2018.

Websites

American Kennel Club: Yorkshire Terrier
https://www.akc.org/dog-breeds/yorkshire-terrier/

Animal Planet: Yorkshire Terrier
https://www.animalplanet.com/tv-shows/dogs-101/videos/yorkshire-terrier

INDEX

Every effort has been made to ensure that these websites are appropriate for children. However, because of the nature of the Internet, it is impossible to guarantee that these sites will remain active indefinitely or that their contents will not be altered.